Contents

Make sure you have a grown-up to help whenever you see this sign.

!

Is it a Minibeast?

Minibeasts are small animals that are often too tiny to be seen with the naked eye. Because there are so many types of animals, zoologists divide them into groups. The two main groups are vertebrates (animals with a backbone) and invertebrates (animals without a backbone). Minibeasts are all invertebrates. Arthropods are the largest group of invertebrates. They include insects, crustaceans, millipedes, centipedes and spiders. Worms are also invertebrates and so are molluscs, a group that includes snails and slugs. Cnidaria are soft water-living minibeasts that include jellyfish.

Caught in Amber

Millions of years ago, some insects were caught in sticky resin that oozed from the bark of pine trees. When this hardened and became amber, the insects were preserved inside.

No Backbone

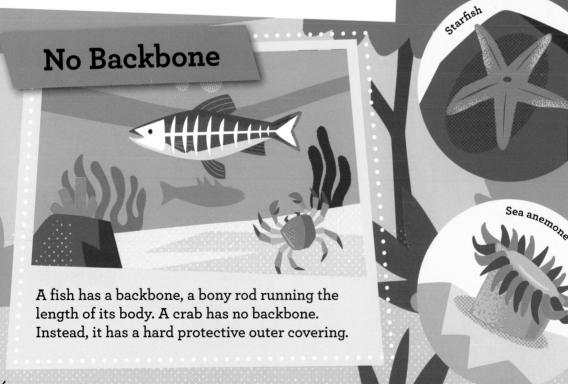

Starfish

Sea anemone

Bee

Earthworm

A fish has a backbone, a bony rod running the length of its body. A crab has no backbone. Instead, it has a hard protective outer covering.

Ants

Ants are tiny minibeasts that can only be seen clearly when looked at under a magnifying glass. This image of an ant is many times larger than life-size.

Minibeasts vary in size, shape and colour. Scorpions and spiders have eight legs, while butterflies, bees and fleas have six, and earthworms and sea anemones have no legs at all. The starfish has a spiny covering, and the snail has a coiled shell that protects its soft body.

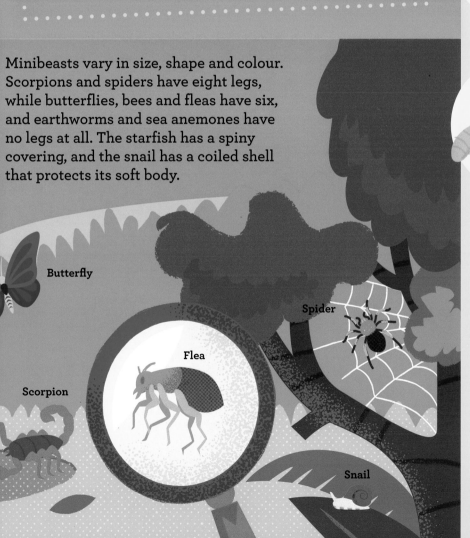

Butterfly

Spider

Flea

Scorpion

Snail

Mollusc (snail)

Arachnid (spider)

Insect (wasp)

Crustacean (woodlouse)

Annelid (worm)

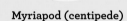

Myriapod (centipede)

Eye-Spy

Minibeasts are found everywhere – in the garden, at the park and on school playgrounds. Try to find an example of a minibeast from each of the main groups. As you try to identify an animal, count the number of legs and look for wings. The pictures above may help with identification.

Growing Up

Caterpillars and butterflies look very different, but they are actually the same animal at different stages in life. In the growing stage, the caterpillar eats plants. Once it's fully grown, it enters the pupal stage. This is when the body of the caterpillar is completely reorganized into the body of a butterfly. After a few weeks, the case of the pupa splits open and the adult emerges. This complete change in appearance is called metamorphosis.

Courtship

When it is time for fiddle crabs to reproduce, the male crab attracts a female by waving his large claw.

The female butterfly lays her eggs on leaves. The eggs hatch within a few days and the young caterpillars feed on the leaves, growing rapidly. After a few weeks they pupate and undergo their metamorphosis.

1. Egg

2. Caterpillar

3. Pupa

4. New adult

5. Adult

DISCOVER IT YOURSELF!

Stick insects are easy to keep as pets.

1. Research first whether a stick insect is the right pet for you. All pets require your time and attention.

2. Stick insects feed on privet and blackberry leaves, so collect some branches for food. Keep the plants fresh by wrapping tissue paper around the bottom of the stems and putting them in a small plastic pot of water.

3. Put in another small pot of water, for drinking.

4. The stick insects may start to lay eggs. The eggs are tiny and are easily confused with droppings. Collect the eggs and keep them in a small container until they hatch.

Eggs

Water

Locust Life Cycle

A locust egg hatches into a small hopper. It looks like an adult, but it is much smaller and lacks wings. The hopper grows rapidly, eating its own body weight in leaves each day. Every few days, it moults its skin to grow larger. At the final moult, the adult locust appears with a set of wings.

Egg

First moult

Second moult

Third moult

Fourth moult

Fifth moult

Adult

Eye-Spy

Female butterflies lay their eggs on the leaves of plants that the caterpillars like to eat. Nettles are popular, and you may find several types of caterpillars feeding on them. Look for caterpillars and make a note of the plants you find them on.

Plant-Eaters

Plants are an important source of food for many minibeasts. Minibeasts and other animals that eat only plants are called herbivores. Most herbivores eat a wide range of plant food, especially leaves, but some feed off just fruit, pollen or nectar. Herbivores are the first link in the food chain because they only feed on plants. In turn, they are eaten by larger animals called carnivores, the meat-eaters.

Honeypot Ants

Honeypot ants store nectar and honeydew in their bodies until they become too large to move.

DISCOVER IT YOURSELF!

See how many minibeasts you can find in the leaves of a tree.

1. Place a large white sheet under a low branch.

2. Give the branch a good shake. All the minibeasts living on that branch will fall onto your sheet.

3. Examine the animals you have caught. Those with wings will probably fly away, but the others will remain. Some of the more common minibeasts you might find are crab and wolf spiders, lacewings, green caterpillars, fruit flies, gall wasps and weevils. There may also be several different types of beetle.

Eye-Spy

Look out for signs of plant-eaters in your garden or school playground – nibbled leaves, white marks produced by leaf miners and oak galls swelling where tiny wasps have laid their eggs.

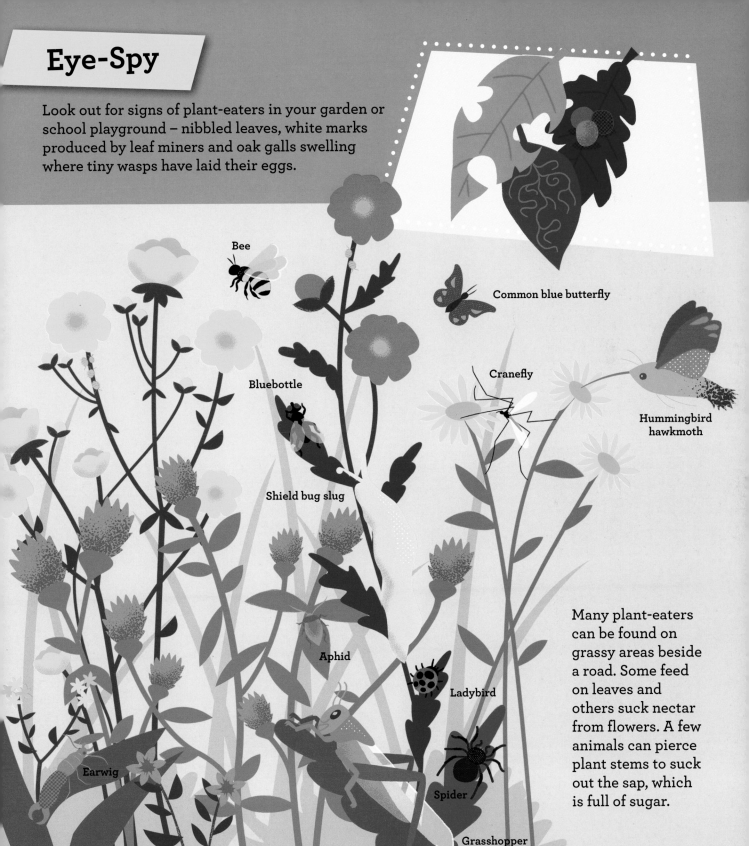

Bee

Common blue butterfly

Cranefly

Hummingbird hawkmoth

Bluebottle

Shield bug slug

Aphid

Ladybird

Earwig

Spider

Grasshopper

Many plant-eaters can be found on grassy areas beside a road. Some feed on leaves and others suck nectar from flowers. A few animals can pierce plant stems to suck out the sap, which is full of sugar.

Mouthparts for Different Foods

The mouthparts of insects are suited to their particular type of food. Butterflies uncoil a long thin proboscis to reach into flowers and suck out the nectar. Grasshoppers have strong biting jaws. Cicadas have piercing mouthparts that are used to suck sap from the plant stem.

Cicada

Butterfly

Grasshopper

Grazing Limpets

Limpets have a rough tongue called a radula, which they use to scrape algae off rocks.

DISCOVER IT YOURSELF!

At night, moths are attracted to bright lights.

1. On a summer night, hang a white sheet on a washing line.

2. Shine a torch through the sheet and watch the moths flying around in silhouette on the other side.

? How It Works

Many moths fly at night in search of food. They are distracted by bright lights and come spiralling into them.

Hunters and Trappers

Hunters and trappers can be found in nooks and crannies of the woodland floor. Beetles and centipedes lie in wait, ready to jump out and chose their pray. The wolf spider lives up to its name!

Many minibeasts feed on other minibeasts. They are called carnivores, or meat-eaters. They are very powerful for their size and are ferocious hunters. Carnivores can move quickly and have good eyesight so that they can spot their prey moving among leaves or flying through the air.

Caterpillar-hunting beetle

Ground beetle

Wood tiger beetle

Wolf spider

Millipede

Centipede

Orb web spider

Mesh web spider

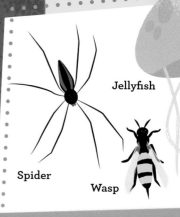
Jellyfish

Spider

Wasp

Poisonous Stings

Jellyfish, spiders and hunting wasps kill their prey with a powerful sting. Hunting wasps carry their prey to their nests to feed their larvae.

Some carnivorous minibeasts set traps to catch their prey. Spiders spin webs with sticky threads to trap and hold flying insects. When an insect gets trapped, the spider bites it and injects a poison that paralyses it. Then it bundles the insect in spider silk and injects it with enzymes that break down its body, turning it to a liquid the spider can suck up.

Nursery web spider

Spiders' Webs

Orb web spiders spin large webs to trap flying insects. Mesh web spiders make webs to trap crawling insects. The nursery web spider spins a net-like web over a plant to protect the eggs she has laid.

DISCOVER IT YOURSELF!

At night, the woods come alive with minibeasts moving about in search of food. You can catch them in a pitfall trap and then return them to the woodland floor.

!

1. Find two plastic cups or other small containers and put one inside the other.

Eye-Spy

Crabs are found on rocky shores, in rock pools and under rocks. See how many you can find on the shore. Remember not to disturb the wildlife and to put something back where you found it if you pick it up.

Aerial Hunters

Dragonflies have large wings and enormous eyes that help them to hunt efficiently. They fly along stretches of water at speeds up to 48 kilometres per hour, looking for flying insects. They pluck their prey out of the air, using their spiky legs as a net.

2. Dig a hole and put both containers in it so that the top of the inside one is level with the ground.

3. Put some meat or fruit in the container. Place a stone across the top, but do not cover it completely.

4. On the next day, lift out the inside container and see what you have caught. Let the minibeasts go.

Runners, Leapers, Creepers

Some minibeasts move across the ground very quickly, while others just crawl. Leaping insects can jump great distances. They have extra long hind legs that give them a powerful take-off. The click beetle escapes from predators by lying on its back and playing dead. Then suddenly it jumps into the air, lands on its feet and runs away. Worms do not have legs, but rely on muscles in their body to move them through the soil in a rippling motion. Snails glide on their muscular foot.

Eye-Spy

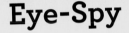

A worm extends its body forwards, then pulls the back part towards the front. See if you can feel the tiny bristles that help the worm to grip the ground as it moves.

Grasshoppers have muscular hind legs that are much longer than the other two pairs. These give the grasshopper a powerful push off when it leaps. Once the grasshopper is in the air, it uses its wings to glide.

DISCOVER IT YOURSELF!

A garden snail moved 31 centimetres in 2 minutes and 13 seconds. Beat this world record by setting up your own snail race.

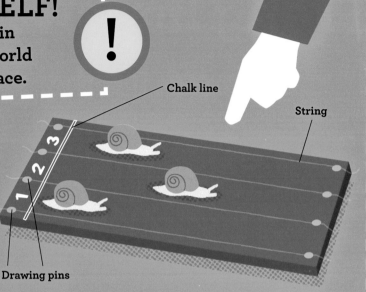

Chalk line

String

1. You will need a board about 1 metre long and 50 centimetres wide. Use string to divide the board into lanes. Hold the string tight with drawing pins. Mark the start line with chalk.

2. Place your snails at the start line and set them off! Once you're finished, carefully put the snails back where you found them.

Drawing pins

Watch Them Move

The best way to watch a snail or a slug move is to place it on a sheet of glass or see-through plastic. Watch it from below so that you can see the rippling movement of muscles in the foot of the animal. As it moves forward, it leaves behind a glistening trail of slime.

Snail

Slug

Looping Caterpillars

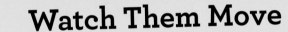

Some caterpillars move in a looping manner. They extend the front of their body forward and then pull up the back end to form a loop.

15

Flying Insects

African giant swallowtail

In the animal kingdom, only birds, bats and insects can fly. Wings allow these animals to travel great distances in search of food. Most flying insects have two pairs of thin wings, but some have just one pair. Beetles have two pairs, but the front pair is hardened to form a tough protective cover for the hind pair, which are folded out of sight. The ladybird has a pair of hard red wings, and underneath are a pair of thin wings used for flight. The fastest fliers are dragonflies, horseflies and hawk moths, which can reach 58 kilometres per hour.

Largest Wings

The world's biggest butterflies belong to the swallowtail family. The African giant swallowtail has a wingspan of about 23 centimetres.

Eye-Spy

Insect wings come in all shapes and sizes. Some have two pairs while others have one. Here are just a few of the different wings that you might spot in the garden or park.

Caddis fly

Lacewing

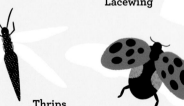

Thrips

Ladybird

Bee

Butterflies have a weak, fluttering flight. Their large wings beat slowly, up and down. The swallowtail butterfly has the slowest wingbeat of any insect, just five wingbeats per second.

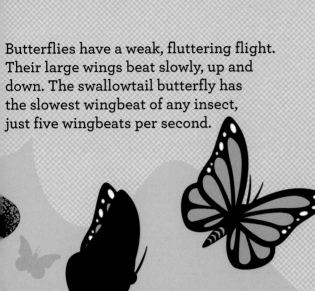

Coming In To Land

A bee will hold out its wings to reduce speed before coming in to land on a flower.

DISCOVER IT YOURSELF!

Attract insects to your windowsill by planting flowers that are rich in nectar and have a strong scent.

1. Fill a window box with compost and water it well.

2. Sprinkle flower seeds onto the surface of the compost. Plant nasturtium seeds near the edge so that they trail over the sides as they grow. Others can be sprinkled in groups.

3. Cover the seeds with a thin layer of compost and wait for them to grow. Water whenever the box looks dry. Then wait to see which insects arrive.

Self Defence

Minibeasts need to be able to defend themselves against predators. Beetles and woodlice have a heavy armour covering that is difficult to crush. Some insects deter their attackers by spraying them with acid or other chemicals. With clever camouflage, minibeasts can lie concealed and avoid being eaten. Their colouring may make them look like a piece of bark, a leaf or part of a flower.

Warning Colours

The bright colours of the sea slug warn other animals that it is covered in sting cells and should not be eaten.

Eye-Spy

Many minibeasts are hard to spot because they are so well camouflaged. Caterpillars may be hidden among the leaves, camouflaged to look like bits of twig. Moths may have wings that are patterned to match the bark on which they rest. Snails may have shells that blend into their background. How many camouflaged minibeasts can you find in your garden or at the park?

Rhinoceros beetle

Some minibeasts have tough outer skeletons. Others have claws or powerful legs. The silkworm caterpillar has dangerous, stinging bristles and the io moth has eyespots to frighten of predators. The scorpion has a sting.

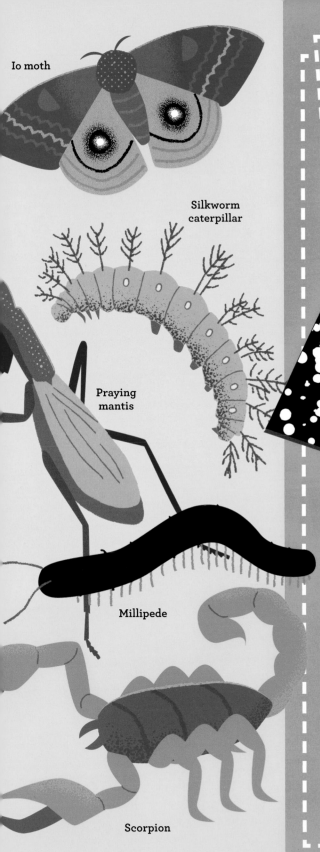

Io moth

Silkworm caterpillar

Praying mantis

Millipede

Scorpion

Try this experiment to see how camouflage works.

1. You will need two pieces of black paper. Cut out a butterfly shape from one piece of paper. Use paint or a pen to make a pattern of white dots on both the butterfly shape and the other piece of paper.

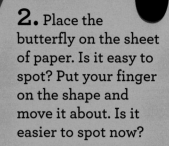

2. Place the butterfly on the sheet of paper. Is it easy to spot? Put your finger on the shape and move it about. Is it easier to spot now?

? How It Works

Camouflage works best when an animal remains still. The camouflage pattern blends into the background. Movement is easily spotted by any predators, even if the camouflage is perfect.

This caterpillar resembles a shrivelled leaf.

Friend or Foe?

Minibeasts live everywhere, indoors and out. Most are harmless, but a few are pests. Slugs, Colorado beetles and locusts damage crops. Leatherjackets, which are the larvae of crane flies, eat the roots of plants, and slugs, snails and caterpillars eat the leaves. Fortunately, there are just as many minibeasts that are useful. Hoverflies and ladybirds help in the garden by eating the aphids that feed on plants. Worms burrow into and aerate the soil and help water to drain away.

Eye-Spy

How many minibeast pests can you find in your garden or local park?

Aphids

Ladybird

Butterfly

Honey bee

Caterpillar

Snail

Garden soil is full of minibeasts. Leatherjackets and beetle larvae live underground until they grow into adult insects. Ants and worms dig tunnels and burrows. The worms and larvae are eaten by birds.

Leatherjackets

Ant

Worm

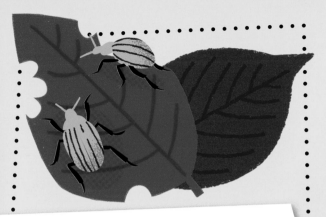

Colorado Beetles

The yellow and black striped Colorado beetle is not very big, but it is a major pest of the potato crop.

A swarm of locusts can devastate a huge area of crops in just a few hours, stripping the plants of all their leaves.

DISCOVER IT YOURSELF!

Try these harmless slug traps in your garden.

!

1. Take half a grapefruit skin, a piece of wood and some black plastic.

2. Place your traps near some vegetables on a warm, wet day when slugs will be active. Leave them overnight.

3. Next morning, see which trap was the most successful. Turn the traps over and let the slugs slide away.

? How It Works

Slugs need moisture, so they prefer places that are dark and damp. The traps create these conditions. The slugs may also try to eat the inside of the grapefruit skin.

Honey Bees

Bees make honey from the nectar they collect from flowers. Beehives are often put in orchards so that the flowers are pollinated by the bees as they look for nectar.

Silk Moths

Silk is made by the caterpillar of the silk moth. When they are ready to pupate, the caterpillars spin a cocoon of silk threads.

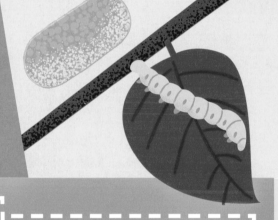

Ladybirds are welcome visitors to our gardens, because they feed on aphids.

DISCOVER IT YOURSELF!

Be a worm charmer.

1. Use string to mark out an area of grass 3 metres by 3 metres.

2. Now persuade the worms to come to the surface by playing music, or prodding the earth with a fork.

? How It Works

Worms like moisture, so they come out of their burrows when it rains. Vibrations trick the worms into thinking that it is raining, so they come to the surface.

Earwig

Woodworm holes

Our homes are a source of food and warmth to minibeasts. The cockroach eats almost anything from crumbs of food to book covers. Microscopic dust mites, each smaller than a full stop, are everywhere. They especially like your bed, where there is a constant supply of dead cells from your skin. Bed bugs inhabit beds, too, and tiny beetles live in the carpets. Woodworms, the larvae of many small beetles, attack wood and leave small holes. Clothes moths nibble holes in woollen clothes.

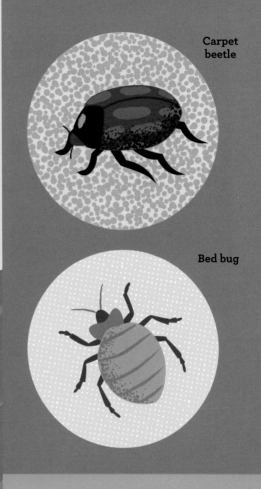

Carpet beetle

Bed bug

If you visit the kitchen at midnight, you may find some unwelcome visitors! Sugary foods attract ants, flies and earwigs. Cockroaches and silverfish feed on crumbs. Lurking in the corners are spiders, waiting to catch their next meal.

Flies

Ants

Spider

Moth

Silverfish

Cockroach

A mosquito pierces the skin and injects a substance that stops blood from clotting, so that it flows freely through the minute hole.

23

Life In the Water

A pool of water is quickly colonized by minibeasts. The first to arrive are the water beetles and mosquitoes, then other insects soon fly in. Ducks may bring the eggs of snails and fish on their feet. Soon the pool is brimming with life. Many microscopic animals swim in the water or live in the mud. In a pond, all animals and plants live together as a community. The water lilies and other plants provide shelter, and food for the plant-eaters.

Water Spider

The water spider spins a balloon-like web that it fills with bubbles of air. It spends most of its time in the air-filled web and darts out to catch prey.

A wide variety of animal and plant life can be found in even the smallest pond. Pond weeds and algae are food for plant-eaters such as mussels and snails. The plant-eaters are food for hunters such as backswimmers, water scorpions and beetles.

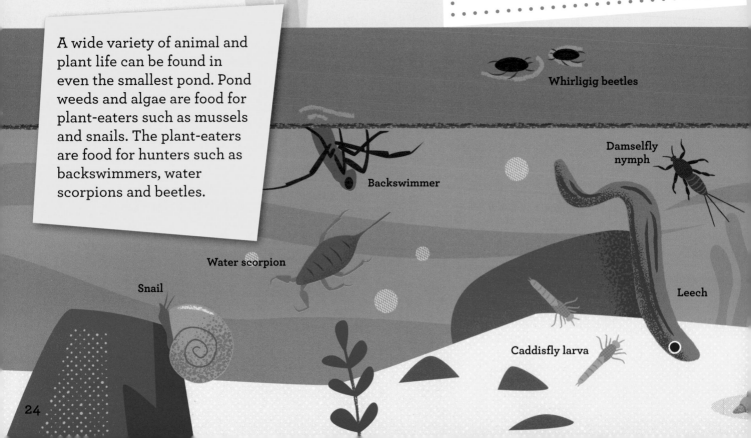

Whirligig beetles

Backswimmer

Damselfly nymph

Water scorpion

Snail

Leech

Caddisfly larva

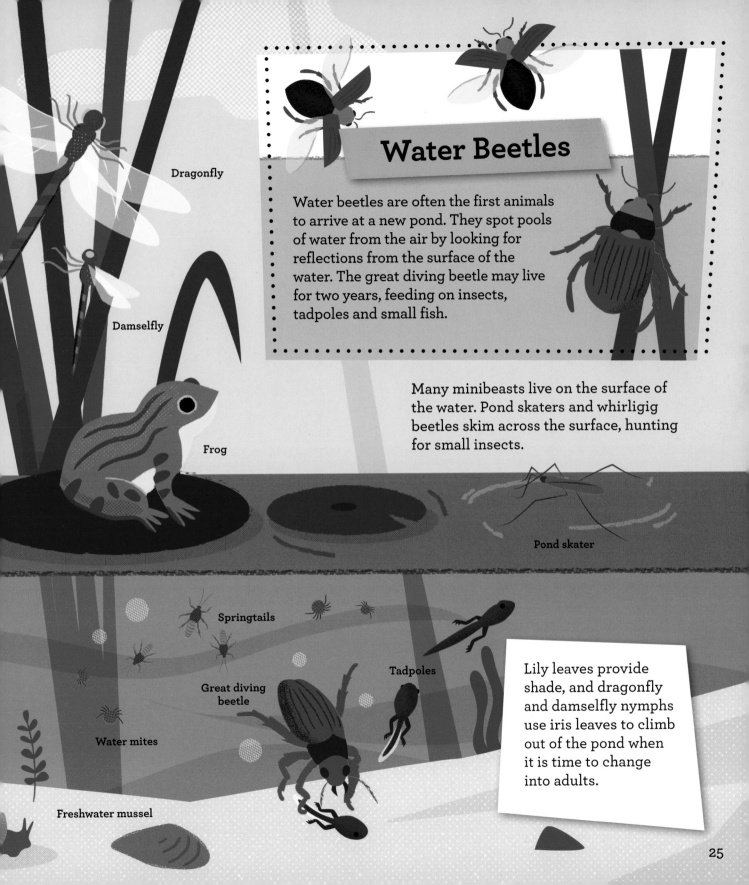

Water Beetles

Water beetles are often the first animals to arrive at a new pond. They spot pools of water from the air by looking for reflections from the surface of the water. The great diving beetle may live for two years, feeding on insects, tadpoles and small fish.

Many minibeasts live on the surface of the water. Pond skaters and whirligig beetles skim across the surface, hunting for small insects.

Lily leaves provide shade, and dragonfly and damselfly nymphs use iris leaves to climb out of the pond when it is time to change into adults.

Dragonfly

Damselfly

Frog

Pond skater

Springtails

Tadpoles

Great diving beetle

Water mites

Freshwater mussel

25

DISCOVER IT YOURSELF!

The best way to find out about life in a pond is to go pond dipping.

!

1. You will need to take a net, a large bowl, some small pots, a magnifying glass and your notebook. You may find a guide book to pond life helpful.

2. Sweep the net through the water to catch the surface minibeasts. Empty the contents into the bowl and examine your catch.

3. You may need to move the animals into the pots to have a close look at them. Try to keep the plant-eaters away from the meat-eaters.

4. Use the magnifying glass to look at the smaller animals. Remember, you may have to count the number of legs to identify an animal.

5. More minibeasts may be found on the pond weed, under lily leaves or on irises near the edge. Others can be found under stones.

6. Note down what you find. The types of minibeast are a good guide to how clean the water is.

7. Return all the animals to the water when you have finished.

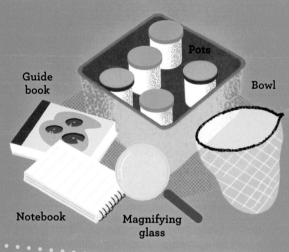

Guide book

Pots

Bowl

Net

Notebook

Magnifying glass

Deep Water Warning

Water is dangerous. Be very careful when working at the edge of the pond. Always take an adult with you.

Life Under Logs and Stones

A pile of logs and dead leaves creates the damp and dark conditions that are ideal for animals such as woodlice and millipedes. These minibeasts play an important role in recycling the nutrients locked up in the remains of dead plants and animals. Beetles, millipedes and woodlice break up leaves into tiny pieces. Other minibeasts eat the rotting wood. Then fungi and bacteria finish the process of decomposition.

Centipede or Millipede?

A millipede has two pairs of legs on each segment, while a centipede has only one pair per segment.

Fallen leaves are broken up by small minibeasts and quickly rot down. Among the leaves and logs are hunters such as centipedes and false scorpions. Frogs and toads may hunt here, too.

Millipede

Centipede

False scorpion

Woodlice

Worm

Springtail

Slug

Woodlice

Woodlice emerge at night to feed on dead leaves and wood. Their bodies are protected with a heavy armour-like covering. Some woodlice can roll up into a ball to protect their vulnerable body organs.

A Recycling Job

Many minibeasts act as rubbish clearing up the remains of dead plants and animals. Flies gather round a dead mouse and lay their eggs on its body. Maggots hatch and feed on the rotting flesh. Soon, all that is left is a pile of bones.

DISCOVER IT YOURSELF!

How many minibeasts can you find in a pile of leaf litter?

1. Collect some leaf litter from a woodland floor. Spread a large sheet of paper on a table and tip some leaf litter onto it. You will quickly spot the minibeasts moving around on the paper. Make sure the larger ones do not run off the edge.

2. Using a paint brush and tweezers, put the minibeasts in little pots to examine them. Try not to mix plant-eaters with meat-eaters.

3. When you have finished, put all the animals back into the litter and return the litter to where you found it.

DISCOVER IT YOURSELF!

Make mini homes for animals in your garden or school playgrounds.

!

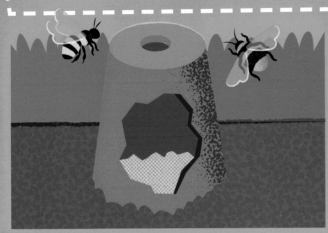

1. A clay pot can make a bumblebee nest site. Put some wood chips or straw inside a clay pot. Then bury the pot upside down in a flower bed, with just the hole showing. Bumblebees may go in through the hole and build a nest.

2. Paper straws can provide a home for small insects. Take a bundle of straws and block one end of each straw with mud, or simply squash them. Then tie the straws together and hang them beneath a window ledge. Soon, small insects will creep into the straws.

3. Pile up logs and stones in a shady place in the garden. The moist and dark conditions will attract beetles, centipedes and millipedes. Frogs and toads may spend the winter in the pile, too.

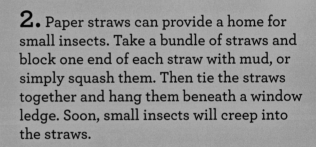

More Things To Try

If you have enough space, you could build a stone wall and earth bank. Stack the stones to form a double-sided wall with space in the centre. Fill the middle with soil, making sure you leave lots of nooks and crannies. Plants will quickly cover the bank, while spiders, woodlice and ants will hide between the stones.

Living Together

Social insects live together in groups or colonies. The colonies form a community in which everyone plays a role. There is usually only one queen, and she is responsible for laying all the eggs. Most of the individuals are workers. Workers are female, and their jobs include building the home, finding food, keeping the home clean and looking after the larvae. There are a few males to mate with the queen. Many bees and wasps live like this, and so do all kinds of ants.

Weaver ants make nests by pulling several leaves together onto a branch and sticking them in place with a glue produced by the larvae.

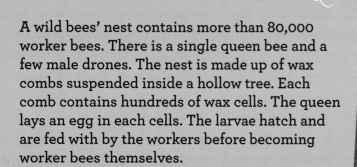

A wild bees' nest contains more than 80,000 worker bees. There is a single queen bee and a few male drones. The nest is made up of wax combs suspended inside a hollow tree. Each comb contains hundreds of wax cells. The queen lays an egg in each cells. The larvae hatch and are fed with by the workers before becoming worker bees themselves.

Eye-Spy

In late summer, look for winged ants on patios and rockeries. These are males and young queen ants that will fly away to start their own colonies.

A termite colony may consist of several million termites. Together, they build a nest using mud glued with saliva. The nest reaches several metres above and below the ground. Hidden within the nest is a maze of tunnels, chambers for larvae, chambers for food and waste and a complex system of ventilation shafts.

Soldier Termites

Soldier termites protect the colony. They attack enemies by injecting a poisonous chemical, or squirting a type of glue.

Ventilation system

Chamber

Queen termite

Tunnel

Index